THE ANATOMY OF CLAY

POEMS

GILLIAN SZE

MISFIT

ECW Press

Published by ECW Press
2120 Queen Street East, Suite 200, Toronto, Ontario, Canada M4E 1E2
416-694-3348 / info@ecwpress.com

LIBRARY AND ARCHIVES CANADA CATALOGUING IN PUBLICATION

Sze, Gillian, 1985–
The anatomy of clay / Gillian Sze.

Poems.
ISBN 978-1-77041-014-5
ALSO ISSUED AS:
978-1-55490-937-7 (PDF); 978-1-55490-984-1 (EPUB)

I. Title.

PS8637.Z425A63 2011   C811'.6   C2010-906833-5

Editor for the press: Michael Holmes / a misFit book
Cover design: David Gee
Cover image: Empty Nest © DNY59
Typesetting: Troy Cunningham
Printing: Coach House Printing 1 2 3 4 5

The publication of *The Anatomy of Clay* has been generously supported by the Canada Council for the Arts, which last year invested $20.1 million in writing and publishing throughout Canada, by the Ontario Arts Council, by the Government of Ontario through Ontario Book Publishing Tax Credit, by the OMDC Book Fund, an initiative of the Ontario Media Development Corporation, and by the Government of Canada through the Canada Book Fund.

Canada Council for the Arts Conseil des Arts du Canada Canada ONTARIO ARTS COUNCIL CONSEIL DES ARTS DE L'ONTARIO

PRINTED AND BOUND IN CANADA

CONTENTS

One:

To Love, To Desire, To Destroy

I affirmed that — for me — personality is a mystery;
— e. e. cummings

FRUITFUL

We speak of nobility
like we can dine on it

We are scared
tatterdemalion
hiding behind organdie

We savour the cool feel
of the spotted jewelweed,
crush the leaves to administer
after playing in poison ivy,
the convenience that the two grow together

We hope that the rest of our lives
could be that propitious

We are good
sometimes

We are all little children still
stopped on the sidewalk
calling,
Wait for me!
just to test our mothers, our fathers,
the validity of ourselves
a good enough reason,

and every possible slant of love.

Two:

Quotidianus

that mysteries alone are significant;
— e. e. cummings

BUN

They love the way she gathers her hair,
her fingers minding her hairline,
combing from the forehead,
down to the temples,
behind the ears.

Yes: she is ordinary, like most people;
but how lucky they are to witness
her miss the last tendril,
the one that sticks to her neck,
curled like a crescent moon.

WATCHING CARS

He lives in an old house beside the hot dog truck stop,
next to the highway ramp leading downtown
with its exits and traffic
and the frequent tremble from a passing semi.

On hot days,
he watches the cars approach:
minivans, U-Hauls and trailers,
each tagged with a different plate.

He's seen them all.

Every day, he waits
to catch sight of a hand out the window,
a pale flash dipping coyly,
waving hello.

As his life unravels,
he thinks back to the hand,
the most beautiful
he's seen all week:
fingers rolling over air,
a silent gesture between engines
so easily missed.

ROSES

It was the kind of morning
the dark never left.
— Stephen Dunn

Clandestine roses have appeared
in her pasta jars and cooled kettles of forgotten water.
They've been stuck in dusty wine bottles,
crammed to the back of her fridge,
strewn across piano keys.
A bouquet in each slipper.
Petals in the toaster.

She blossoms onto the subway
and unfolds rosebuds from her pockets.
A boy tows potted roses behind him on his skateboard.
The scent cuts the underground desert,
the forlorn winter,
the fog.

HURON

If this street were a grocery aisle,
you'd reach the end
basket empty.

The roofs sag their shoulders,
the tired look of seated,
slouched men.

The branches play cat's cradle
with a stray piece of plastic,
a muddied and dry game.

The iron fence sprouts from dirty snow,
a new coat of paint dried dripping,
a rushed draping to hide something.

THE NIGHTGOWN

A young girl
mends an old white nightgown
by the open window.

She only has black thread.
She tries to make neat, tiny stitches.

There is no breeze.
She sweats with her head bowed
and the musty nightgown
breathes back.

WE CAN DROWN IF WE CLOSE THE DOORS

He's gotten used to painting portraits
of the girls he's dated
in tears;

they've been crying on his walls;
the floors are always wet;
the mop is weary.

The faces change:
some round like oranges,
others like watermelon seeds
turned upside down,

but they all have crinkled chins
            leaky corks

and they cry in harmony
as the words sink
to the backs of their throats.

THE TAKEN WIFE

These evenings
you find more joy in the television
than in me:
your face an empty dish.

Tonight's show,
a woman tells her daughter:
your life becomes what you pay attention to.

I remind myself to use jasmine lotion
after I emerge from the shower
and yet, each morning,
I fail to do so.

Domesticity is more than
the cup of coffee
I set at your side
as you listen, one ear to morning news,
the other to the traffic.

It is the distortion
that takes place when all that's left
is the cooling stovetop,
a dripping shower,
a mix-up between
compassion and *compression,*
the latter felt
with each plunge of the French press,
each squeeze of a package of brown sugar.

Before you come home,
I wash,
tumble dry on low,
and fold myself into your drawer.

DUNDAS & CRAWFORD

She waits in flip-flops for the bus.
It's ten a.m. and zero degrees;
her socks are ripped at the heels
and she holds her cigarette close to her mouth,
her elbow up in thought.

A tired housecoat falls away at her shoulders.

Once, surely, there was a man
who loved to watch the way her body bent
when she opened the dishwasher,

how she looked in the morning,
her silhouette as she unfolded from the bed,
stretched
and brought a half-bottle of wine to her lips.

Her hair, tumbled in knots,
is still tied to that.

The bus comes, she presses on
and the door closes on the sidewalk,
on the series of old men filing by
with their jackets open.

GREEN ROBIN HOOD

He can't stand anyone
who doesn't take care of their things —
house owners who neglect their lawns,
people who don't walk their dogs.

A pie is always best
when the plums are grown in your yard
and hand-picked.

And that potted plant
you placed beside your front door
won't see the cold in late September
when it is stolen from your steps.

AFTER A DOCTOR'S APPOINTMENT

The sun stains the sky like pink grapefruit
from one end to the other,
discolours our eyes.

We pass the poplars he planted last year.
The bony trees stand small
until we get closer;
looking up,
the leaves blink in and out,
opening and closing to only more green.

The garden has brought up weeds.
They veil the small cucumbers
and watermelons
still waiting to swell.
When we go further down the road,
the sun follows
then stops, tired, and drops.

The flowers have fallen off the sumacs,
their bodies lie pink, soft and scaly like fish.

A pair of large white birds fly past.
He claims they are storks
before we realize
that they are only herons
flying away from the sun.

CIGARETTE

A woman sits by the window
of her third-floor apartment.
She wears white shorts
and smokes,
flicking cinders
with the thin wrist of a flautist.

She taps ashes down
to the corner of Guilbault and St. Laurent,
down past the windows of Bedo Outlet,
to the street where the pavement was once hit
with rain,
where just shortly before
the clouds threw their entire weight against the earth.

But now, the pavement is drying,
St. Laurent the faint scent of wet dog;
the sale rack is rolled back out to the sidewalk,
bright blue dresses,
fifteen dollars.

GETTING OFF AT BAY STATION

Trepidation smears
the boy's mouth.

His hand grips a hand,
mindful of the gap.

DIVINING

She reads cracks in the pavement,
steps gingerly over the lines,
the road stretched
like a palm.

Her oversized rubber boots
slap the backs of her calves.

She is learning to be vigilant,
looks for meaning in every striation.

She frequently dreams of turning to stone
and, petrified,
people visit her. She tells them,
If you can count the tears
and collect them in a jar,
I can tell you why I cry for you,
and where you hurt the most.

She was always told not to be nosy.

She is tired of surprises,
the alarm without origin.
She's read that tigers don't usually
attack from the front.
She's gotten used to sleeping on her back.

Oh, if you knew, she says to no one.

The nearby cliffs are alive
only when the tide's in.
Ahead, the town nestles in water.
From here, everything looks like clay.
Each dash of straw in the fields
is lying to somebody.

DEMONS IN THE DARK

Something wakes her,
drags her from her bed to the kitchen.
She pours herself a glass of milk
and forgets it.

Outside the moon is low,
hanging in the jingle of streetlights.
The clusters circle the city's wrist.

A cat makes its way up a roof,
pauses when a television flickers on.

She makes her own way back to bed,
steps carefully over the light
which, earlier,
came in through her window,
turned once,
and crumpled to the floor to sleep.

FLORAL

Every night since moving here
she's watched the man next door
in his kitchen
talk to his plants.

She's scared
that her mother has forgotten her,
and she can't remember her dreams anymore;
they've drowned
like those kittens her mother once collected in a pillowcase
and plunged into a bucket of water.

She stares as his mouth moves.

Hello geraniums.
Hello zinnias.

ONCE MORE

The funeral was four years ago,
but every year I find my brother
in the shed where we store the lawnmower,
the wood steeped in
last summer's grass.

He cradles a bottle to his chest
and he cries for a woman who left
and fell in love with death —
six months later,
whipped into an affair
that no pleading could cut loose.

The next morning,
the hangover holds him;
he says her name once more
before making coffee,
and I can hear the longing
stand before us in the kitchen
not knowing what to do.

LEAVING COUNTRYSIDE

A yellow finch is dead on Canborough Road,
its eyes open to passing traffic.

Over the bridge, killdeer birds, disturbed,
fly from the shaded water: a skimming disorder.

Like flies on an open sore, geese gather on small islands.
A scabbed world through a bus window glows yellow.

ROUTE 515

She is there every night at 9:08,
four stops before his route ends.

The aisle is always clogged,
so she stands near him,

gripping the pole.
Signs of a crowded bus

show on her face
in the rear-view mirror.

This summer,
he was early just once,

and he didn't pull from the curb,
even when feet carped the ground.

He just watched her
run past the dumpster

and, under the streetlight,
like a loose piece of paper,

fly straight through
his door.

TRAINING

It's November and it just started to rain.
You sit in the back seat of the taxi,
watch the thin peel of a leaf
stick to the windshield.

The driver rambles on about love,
how, at thirty, he could pluck
any woman he wanted
off the disco floor.
He demonstrates: his hand snatches
then returns to his chest,
a fistful of nothing.

He looks up in the mirror,
asks if you are married,
and you shake your head.
He grunts and says that he's been married twice.
A second marriage is okay, he says,
his head leaning to the right
as he makes a left into the train station.
With the first, you never know what you want.
The first is all about lust.
But the second, the second is okay.

The sound of your rolling luggage
shadows you as you head to the doors.
You're still toting decade-old love letters
from your ex
and you don't know why.

It's still early morning.
The day grows older with each person
passing where you sit, straight in your chair.

Winter is delayed this year.
Your train is ahead of time.

INSOMNIAC CONJECTURES

The dark has stolen my sleep again,
thrown it, like a deranged sweater, over the wooden owl
perched on the edge of my neighbour's balcony
with the half-closed barbecue
and empty terracotta pots.

A house can grow bored, but doesn't sleep.

I move with it,
find myself in the kitchen with a dirty mug
stained with a slow drip that never made it to the bottom,
the tea leaves dried, prickled to the sides.
Who knew the savageness of tea leaves?

In bed, I rearrange restlessness
but I can't explain the paranoia.
I want to be indispensable, like blood,
and craved, like an extra hour in the morning.

The shadow of the fire hydrant spilling over the curb
startles me.

A cat stares at my shadow in the bushes,
his head twitching as I pass the window
and I wonder why he doesn't look up,
if he's blind,
or if there's something more honest about me
when I'm not there.

I want to spy on my neighbours,
but it's too dark to make out their bodies.
I flip through books instead.
The world is ugly,
and the people are sad, Wallace Stevens whispers.

Tell me about it, the wooden owl says,
as he swivels his head backwards
to look at me.

DELILAH IN SEVEN PARTS

I.

Since leaving Thomas and moving to the city, Delilah makes a point of visiting the post office every afternoon after lunch. She asks the post girl with the light freckles and wide smile for a single local stamp. Delilah knows that it's a simple request, something easy for the post girl to remember. It's not like Starbucks and ordering a latte with a series of variables. And Delilah doesn't write letters — the same way she doesn't drink coffee — but it's nice all the same, to show up and have the post girl recognize her, rip off a stamp, just know exactly what Delilah wants. And each time, Delilah pops it into her coin purse. It's getting full. The coins no longer have space to make a single sound.

II.

Delilah's hometown is a small, polite place. It's so small that she once spent her birthday with just her friend, Sally. Delilah was starting to date Thomas that year but he never showed up. And Sally, she was so polite that, for a gift, she gave Delilah a book titled *How to Discover a Cheater*. Delilah laughed when she saw it, put it down on the table and asked Sally if she was ready for cake — which Delilah had baked herself that afternoon — and Sally, politely, declined.

III.

The city still scares Delilah. She lives on her own in a small apartment, across the street from a strip club. Her neighbour downstairs is a boy in his twenties who is always topless. He often fixes his bike outside and Delilah peeks through the curtains and looks down at his shoulders. She doesn't understand how his body can be so uniformly golden. Once, he glanced up and waved. She ducked. She sat on the floor, her thirty-two-year-old heart pounding like that time when she was younger and she hid in her room after her mother discovered what she called "dirty books" in her knapsack.

IV.

Thomas asked Delilah to marry him a couple days after she told him that she was pregnant. In the photos, Delilah is wearing a white dress that goes a little past her knees. She is smiling; *like the sun is going to burst out of your mouth,* her mother would say. Thomas doesn't smile in the pictures. In fact, he looks bored. But Delilah loved it, didn't see it as bored at the time. It was just how he looked. Ordinary, with his brown eyes and brown hair and broad face. When Sally was introduced to him, Delilah later asked, *Isn't he handsome?* Sally just said, *He kinda looks like a squash.*

v.

Delilah lost the baby two months in. She doesn't like the details and tries to forget most of them. All she knows is that shortly after, Thomas stopped coming home at night. Sometimes he'd be gone for two whole days. Delilah started reading the book Sally gave her and would write Post-it notes to herself that she'd stick to the bottom of her underwear drawer. She would write out pieces of advice like, *How to discover a cheater: search his car;* or *How to discover a cheater: bring him close and note any peculiar scents.*

After Thomas came right out and told her, Delilah locked herself in the room, chopped off her hair so it hung just below her ears in jagged locks and packed her belongings in her suitcase. When she got to the bottom of the drawers, her eyes were so wet that they stained everything incomprehensible. She couldn't even read her own writing: *How to dislover a cheater.* It didn't really matter though. She realized later that they were both saying the same thing.

VI.

Now Delilah lives in the city and doesn't know anybody the same way they don't know her. In her building, everybody's first name begins with someone else saying: *So I heard that . . .* Delilah often wonders what people heard about her but stops herself because she can't stand the possibilities of what she isn't. Everyone knows about the woman next door, the lady in her fifties who wears too much eye makeup. It's said that she visits the porn theatre every Saturday night when movies are free for couples. She sits in the back wearing only a fur jacket. Opens it when the men approach, their bodies peaked and bursting before they reach her.

Delilah fears that she'll end up like her.

VII.

Delilah gets on the subway and loves it. She watches the people fall asleep and stumble in their seats. She almost wishes someone would watch her so keenly but she doesn't want to look graceless with her head limp on her neck so she tucks her head in her folded arm and fixes herself against the window. She dreams that the post girl trims her hair so it's all even, smiles wide, her freckles dancing in recognition and says, *That will be fifty-two cents.*

The subway makes its stop. The neighbour from downstairs gets on and seats himself behind her. Now they are sitting back to back and Delilah is fully awake. She notes that he is wearing a shirt. Delilah looks at her own reflection for a long time before flicking to the other form beside her. Their gaze thickens and sets on the glass for a couple seconds before shattering it.

ELEGY I

Because there is only so much shelter
in a painted door, one day you open it
and you're faced with an impugning gale.
It blows you out to the sky
and the whole world
slows.

There is a secret up here,
you're certain.
Up here,
you can confirm whether Beethoven
really dunked his head in cold water to stay awake,
or the Trojan horse was worth all the hearsay,
or whether Death stops at your toes.

You want the painted door back.
You drew it to get to the next room.
But looking down,
even the waves of the river's current
jump at you
like startled eyebrows.

10/18/09

A finished espresso crusts the afternoon

someone tosses popcorn out the passenger window
and pigeons ignore traffic

the raised pant leg of a cyclist bares
a Herculean calf, just as it presses on the pedal

a puppy leads the way

deserted ice sits outside the grocery store;
bits of broccoli find their way through as it melts

someone buys yesterday's newspaper

a man grieves for his father

the fossilized tire print becomes brittle in mud

the sun throws a milky gaze over
all that pales.

THE RIGHT TENOR

The memory he keeps around his neck
is of the light
blinking outside his father's hospital room.

Even if he could try to enter again,
I tell him that it would never change.
Death tapers quickly to nothing
like the tine of a snake's tongue.

I want to provide a precise percentage
of people who pass in the absence of family —
a statistical source of comfort,
or maybe a phrase
culled from daytime talk shows:
You will get past this,
or,
You must forgive yourself first.

•

In Goa,
he scattered his father's ashes
in the ocean. He and his mother
wept. Then he and his brother
swam, smelled incense.

Closure is a myth,
he would tell me months later.
An imagined fragrance,

burned, and then gone,
replaced by salt,
swindled gratitude.

•

In his mother's home,
we sleep in his old room.
I ask him what trees grow in his backyard;
their shapes, foreign in the dark,
fork into a moonlit sky.
Spruce, birch, oak and pine.
Really?
No. I know we have a pine tree though.

•

His father's dead
but he brings him back:
the way he misplaces his glasses,
his ability to plant himself on the couch,
read for hours.

The aftermath has made him
afraid of people.

He prefers to stay inside
where his books are,
the television buzzing,

my love just down the hallway.

•

I don't recognize him in my sleep anymore

yet in the mornings,
when he calls me closer,

even sleep doesn't stop me
as I roll
until I reach his side of the bed;

he could be anyone.

•

I dream of a boy,
who looks like a younger him,
narrow and still growing into his ears.

He asks me to define the word: *undo*.

The next day, I have an urge
to write something
where I use the word *tragic*,
easily, naturally,
without bringing in heaviness
or theatrics, or what it really means:

tragikos: something pertaining to goats.

If that's even possible.

•

At his mother's, before the prayers,
we fill a golden bowl with apples,
pomegranates, bananas, mandarins, plums.
The flowered garlands, made too small,
need to be untied, taped to the portraits.
Fresh from the fridge,
the carnations are clammy, cold, dying.

In the basement
I find him rummaging behind the bar,
plucking empty bottles to test volume.
He finds a corkscrew, the handle
shaped like a boy.
The metal spiral, his penis.

He laughs, uncontrollably,
corkscrew in hand, as if to unscrew
an imaginary trapdoor above him.

I think to use the word *tragic*,
even though this moment doesn't pertain to goats.
I think I will laugh along,
even though I don't get what's funny.

•

Our hair still smoky from prayers,
we lie in bed, as if two cliffs.
His back to me,
I know by the light on his bare arm
that he is awake,
and we grow small,
a cliff each, a whole water away.

Be kind, I say,
with a vague notion of what it is
I am trying to mean.
I should have used other locutions:
You will get past this.
You must forgive yourself first.

Be more specific, he replies,
words sinking into the pillow.

I sit up, prepared for one of his sighs,
or, *What now?*
I would tell him that I am looking at the trees,
finding a way to describe them:
strands of hair,
fishing rods and shadows on a wall,
a polygraph.

He lies there,
leaves the curtains open;

we will be convinced
it's just so we can see the moon,
so the morning light can come in
wake us more easily,
but it's probably more
to make clear the incomprehensible,
to air out the grief.

THIS IS HOW YOU TURN THE SOIL

This is how you brush your teeth and how you tie your shoes. Watch how mommy pours the milk — with one hand holding the cup. This is how you part your hair and braid each tail yourself. This is how you wash your hands after coming in from play. This is how you fold your shirts: sleeve-to-sleeve and tucked inside the body. This is how you peel a Band-Aid so it's wrapped tight around your finger. This is how you use your indoor voice. This is how you say no. And this is where you wait for me to pick you up from school: right in front, by the only red brick in the wall.

This is how you place a pad, centring first before peeling off the tabs. This is how you press your lips together to spread the colour evenly. This is how you buy a jacket and where you tuck your hand along the lining, right by the left breast. This is where you blow to see if it will resist the wind. This is how you sew on a button, through the two holes and over and over. This is how you gut a fish; it can't hear you, and its heart is dead between your fingers. This is how you wrap a present. This is how to take a group photo without capturing too much ceiling. This is how you turn the soil to pluck out the carrots that have been hiding all season. This is how you shift gears from second to third to fourth.

This is how you fold your clothes and pack a suitcase. This is how to clean your own bathroom and paint your walls, in old comfortable clothes. This is how you buy your own cutlery. This is how you skin a chicken, the knife piercing the film that hems the fat. This is how it feels to fall in love — sharp and sudden like breaking a bone. This is how you hold your baby, her head in the crook of your arm or in the palm of your hand. This is how you change a diaper, the baby tummy-side up before fastening the tabs in front. This is how to spread the almond oil to soothe your breasts when they are sore from feeding.

This is how to do the laundry when dinner is burning on the stove and baby is wailing in the crib. This is how to cry like you just learned how. This is how it sounds in the middle of the night. This is how to wait. This is how you tuck yourself into bed. This is how you learn to stop pouring an extra glass of wine. This is how to sign the papers and get used to an old name. This is how you tuck her in, letting her flip the pages of the story. This is what to say when she asks where daddy is. This is how far down you can cut your heart before it splits completely. This is how to re-order the photo albums when she's asleep and you're alone, sitting on your living room floor. This is where you hide those papers. This is how you cry. This is how to break gracefully. This is how you tuck yourself in at night.

HIGHWAY 132

Heartache is just beneath your hand
as you steer down this road.
The soybean fields are lush now;
you've seen them every week this season
driving out to the country.
Weekdays, you are a bachelor
with a single-room apartment you never clean
but at night your body is still fifty
and refusing regret.
This is the turn where someone
— probably some immigrant —
is building his home.
A huge Victorian on a huge plot.
Each week the small shack
at the south-east corner
is torn down a bit more
and the new house swells
with windows and brick.
Today the shack is gone,
like it gave birth to the house
and abandoned it
(this house that has more rooms
than people you know
who would answer your call and say,
Yes, I'll stay with you a night).
You sleep in the old adobe place
by the St. Lawrence
where the curtains drape over the couch
like faint ghosts.
Tomorrow, you will take the boat out.

Fish are hungriest in the morning,
your father told you.
Under the yeasty sun,
the water will come after you
thick and whipped like a wedding train.
Turn off the engine now.
Watch the water return to somnolence.
Watch and wait.

FIRST HYMN

Cædmon, sing me hwæthwugu.
— Bede

Now we must rave the somatic reaping:
the stomach of summer and another sun's labour,
the winding of wheels, the formula to woman.
Even fall's failings have more to foster:
the remaining milk to make cheese in winter,
the glut of grapes for another time's garnet wine,
leftover love — smoked, cured, preserved, pickled — look to it later.
What our tongues tested, made afterwards
firm ground for something that worked, we'll forget just how well.

Three:

Extimacy

and that love is the mystery-of-mysteries
who creates them all
— e. e. cummings

WAKE UP

We are all born part mistake.
It shows, like how a child looks more like his mother
as he grows older.

Two people with the right genes,
will each wake the next day, thinking,
I made us a terrible memory.

One will describe the pain like a sword
that pierces diagonally through the torso;
the other will push on his back to get it out.

I made us a terrible memory.
I wash my white shirt the next morning
in the bathroom sink.

I wear black as I scrub. I am grieving
over dirty cotton, grass stains,
all of yesterday that ever happened.

When you sat in the shower stall
with your head sad on your knees,
I stood watering you, waiting for you to grow.

FIDDLEWOOD

I've been looking for you in a drizzled forest,
chewing its damp edges and twigs,
sucking balled dew through my teeth.

The moss has tamed me
but I still dream at night.
You are the moon-man that lights on my face.
You are the cause for the ache in my neck.

I scrape mould just to remake edibility,
put safely into my mouth;
like you,
my world's gone bad.

If the sun comes,
I'll dry.
We're small.
The slightest causes are tremendous,
full-bodied and swift.

The earth turns her head,
looks over a shoulder
and everything is changed.

MOSES POINT, 10/08

for alison

The ferry pulls in and October laps the hull clean of water.
You pick me up at Swartz Bay, my stomach afloat in water.

Moses Point still gasps from the storm. You cut the engine.
    Leftover rain
drips from Japanese maples as if their crowns were once
    underwater.

Back home, you've returned to smoking in secret. By mid-
    afternoon,
you've stamped out your second, kicked it into a neighbour's
    puddle, mid-water.

We edge down the hill to the end of the yard, past the tree
    house
your father built and your brother's garden, unwatered.

These trees have always lived here: the peeling arbutus, the
    harvest
of pears, apples, plums, figs, hazelnuts. The roses have mouths
    full of water.

Down by the shore, we find washed-up jellyfish the size of
    records.
They'll die, you say plainly. Their viscid bodies quiver for water.

We discover a swing made with a smooth log tied to thick ropes
and take turns grasping that space above water.

You teach me your home, this place that knew you before I did.
After dinner we go down to glimpse the phosphorescence in the
    water.

From the dock we clap Deep Cove with twigs, pinecones and
    bits of bark.
This smell can make me cry, your voice dim and watery.

A brief light. It's too late in the year. But the moon shows us
a seal lift his head a moment from the water.

21st AVE.

When we moved in
the thin walls were a single note
on a reed flute.

Their white echoes lingered on the palate,
a painted taste of metal at the back of the throat.

The rooms took their fill:
a musty couch,
a grandfather clock, thick as chocolate,
a bowl of blood oranges,
our frosted white bed —
and the house narrowed its mouth,
became a sibilant bird.

Over the years,
we coated the walls;
each sound stuck:
a clanging pan,
our fervent knocking,
shuffling slippers,
the yeasty rise of pillows in early afternoons,
I'm home,
the curdled ringing of the phone,
love,
empty nights.

Now we pack
to walk out to our separate trucks
and the walls are thick and loud,

but each belonging silenced in boxes
only strips the quiet air

until we are standing barefoot, framed in rice paper:
I, my hair piqued with sweat,
You, wearing a summer dress and holding a hammer,
the rooms mocking in their final symphony.

CATS

You tell me about the poisoned cats
that showed up on the front lawn
where you stayed in Gulu.

The area was overrun with them
so the hotel owner put poison in the garbage,
but not enough. You woke up
with fifteen cats foaming and howling
outside your window.

We walk over to Oak Bay
and B.C. is as you left it. The sky
is unpredictable, the rocks haven't moved,
the same water pushes itself towards you.

You confess it's beautiful
but after all you've seen —
kids dying from malaria,
kids with names like
Mercy, Innocence, Fortunate —
you've learned to describe home as *monotonous*.

How are we to know what to do
when we are far, when we return?

The next morning,
wondering how to kill fifteen cats swiftly,
the women of Gulu
picked up the trembling bodies with sticks
to drown them
laughing at you the whole time.

CROSSING BORDERS

. . . agnosco veteris vestigia flammae.
— Virgil

There are laws we abide
when with certain people
(like entering another country).

We are consistent in everything we avoid;
practice over time
has led us to pick speech like flowers.
We learn all their names.

Here,
like everywhere else,
we soak them in water
so they die
just a little bit slower.

FASHION BIZ

It's a hard fit to find
with these women
who walk down the corridor
like they are swimming,
arms floating,
eyes inspecting their legs
with each step.

It's a quick strip;
when I hold out my arms,
they teach me my bust
measure by measure,
measure me wrong.

DEAD-WALKING

A single season may strike campfires in a man's blood. [. . .]
Few men may come back from the dead for you.
— Mary di Michele

Gone,

he tells me that he would come back from the dead for me.
It is a long trip, and I am not old enough to be sure
I am worth all that trouble.

My mother says that we are only afraid of ghosts
if we are marked by bad conscience —
the ghosts can smell it — every wrong in our bodies.

I must stink of it.
And mother knows she is right;
she is barely surprised to learn I've grown up
to sleep with a light on.

•

When his voice breaks
I am cracked open. I shine out from the splinters,
how angels appear to the good and dying.

I am more like a click beetle, luminescent but hardly saintly.
I shed my skeleton when he is wounded,
play nurse, soothe.
I swear I mean it.

But touch me in tropical forests and ordinary days,
watch me fall on my back
and play dead.

•

It is nothing but a curiosity, my history,
even to me. Who doesn't ever wonder
what happened after? To ask, *So how exactly did you survive
without me?*

When I left, he ran alongside the bus
like in a movie. Except I didn't see him —
he told me later.

In the mirror, I strip
and my body excites me like it isn't even mine.
I am studying someone else's spine,
the rise and fall
of a backside.

He isn't here
but I know that he can see the radiance
simmering beneath my skin, a small light

sufficient for reading, for hunting ghosts.

FORCED RETIREMENT

I am an Engineer, in my profession I take deep pride. To it I owe solemn obligations.
— "The Oath of the Order of the Engineer"

For thirty years
you ate porridge in the morning,
laid a knife, quietly,
across a plate of bread crumbs.

Some days,
I'd wake to the sound of you in the kitchen,
an opus of ordinary objects:
the clink of the scraped jam jar,
the stick of the fridge door,
and always that chipped white chair
scuffing the floor.

The scare is over now;
they handed you a letter last Monday,
escorted you out.
I try not to imagine your face,
old and defeated;
pretend I don't know
that when it comes to dealing with pain
I am just as proud as you are.

Instead,
I think of that man from my childhood,
crimson and furious,
running after me in the hall.

You said you were lucky
when they didn't lay you off ten years ago;
instead, you were just re-located —
around the same time that riot broke out
at Headingley jail.
Every day for a year,
you drove an hour to Stonewall
to *play with planes.*

When everyone brought a child to work
I sat with you on that hour-long drive
and we went through Stony Mountain
where you passed the penitentiary
at least two times a day,
and how you must have thought of it
years later, when our doors were locked
and you never tried the knob more than twice.

LOCATED

The night is unfit
but no longer a surprise.

You have said it yourself:
tonight, she is enough for what you need.

In bed,
I lie awake
and behind my eyelids
are passing clouds,
the brief shelter of a stranger's umbrella,
the way one would imagine what it meant
for another to *move on*,
like a train waning to a point between two hillsides,
          a movement,
the further quiet when a door shuts in the dark.

In the middle of the night,
I wake without breath
          and write my name over and over again
                    to keep myself from disappearing.

MY PSYCHE

You are asleep,
imperfect in your smooth nightshirt,
its seams crisp from the wash.
Hair freshly combed,
you sleep posed
as if someone would paint you,
the thin band of your arm
across the pillow.

Outside
a woman laughs loudly at the night.

I prefer you in the mornings,
numb beneath the dawn's burden
and then the flicker.
Half asleep,
skin rumpled and perfect.

The woman laughs once more,
twitches the black curtain
in understanding.

FLUTTER BUG

The flutter bug never made it. I just wanted to say.
It baked in the old Buick beside the closed window,
staring out, a withered light lint.

I thought of it on my way to see you
while waiting for the streetcar on Spadina,
across from the Scott Mission and the Waverley Hotel
where men tested their strength by jerking on spindly trees.

You, dark Warhol girl in high-waisted jeans, delivering a letter.
I slept in the braids you gave me, slept in a waning summer
where you and the city were just a perhaps happening.

We cleaned the hours, tidied the minutes
until there was no time left.
Then I unknotted myself in the morning,
woke to a bird that sobbed like a child.

BLOOD SIGN #2

Ana Mendieta smells like mud and wildflowers.
She stands beside me as we watch her on the TV screen
lower herself to the ground, drag her painted hands
down a wall.

There's wet grass stuck to her thighs,
a cold, burnt stench.

The video plays over and over.
Ana with her arms raised,
sinking to her knees,
then walking away.
Her eyes, pixelated, observe me.

She's made it out of the canal,
that dripping red outline of her fall,
the final result,
the spot from where she stepped out
and is now quietly beside me.

This self-made mark,
an edict, lingers seven seconds longer.

How many of us have fallen
into water while trying to catch the moon
or during a waxen flight sunwards?

In Winnipeg, a fifteen-year-old once scribbled:
I want to write something
so moving

one will question and then change his religion.
Who knew I'd be so afraid and fascinated
with the suffocating splash.

Ana leaves the gallery.
Her wet prints follow after her.
Here I am.
I was here.

I watch the exit sign
shine red and steady above the door.
You want that too,
she had smiled as she withdrew.

JARS OF IVY

You had no trouble ripping me apart.
You capped portions of me into jars
and like a mad scientist, talked to me as if I were a plant,
flourishing beneath your voice, the sound of you making the air
fecund. My breasts, your little miracles. You said they mocked
  gravity
and then the rest of me did too, staying afloat in fluvial
  trappings.
The god of bounty knew the god of poverty
and Love sprung from between them to tell us that there would be
no more evolution. Love will lavish and impoverish for always
and when you winked at me, one of my eyes, on its own,
  blinked back.

I feed myself gin in the mornings. Toped, I no longer have a sense
of what's missing. Whatever parts you never returned, I've
  replaced,
sewn on with calumnies. My schefflera plant is dying and I can see
you wrapped in its trunk as it darkens. Leaves take the shape of
  your grin.
Smiles fall from the dead weight of teeth. But the ivy is hardy
and I scoop it from its roots with a tablespoon, wash the soil off
and stick it in old jars. Give it a spot by the window.
This is a new sort of Darwinism, I think as I watch my hands
return to the pot, spoon ready. Keep that which is salvageable,
that which survives in plain water, that which still moves with
  the sun.

ANIMA

My seven-year-old nephew
tells me that he is fourteen
in shark years.

I bark twice.

The whale has me beat.
It knows six different sea languages,
and I, on land, know two.

One day, I tell him,
you'll stare at someone
and all expression will be lost.

A linguist can attest.

How are we all not the same,
as we lie here like cows
waiting for rain?

Somewhere

a fox
screams
like a woman.

LEAVING WINNIPEG

Winter here distresses the ankles.
The tarsus snaps in frost
and we are elapsed
in this cold place,
as if bare feet never vaunted in sand.

There are beaches,
but I've already forgotten the way.

By the church,
men wrapped in neon
climb under the roads to work on pipes,
only their eyes showing;
the first view: a cloud of breath.
Metal cylinders pylon the streets,
snow sticks to the windy side.

The wind brings little change.

On Pembina,
I drive past a sign outside the funeral home:
Immediate cremation.
$995.
No hidden costs.
The Palomino Plains Motel has jacked up its prices
to forty-nine dollars a night.

Looking down from the plane
I know exactly who I don't want to be:
that guy with clunky boots

loading luggage when it's forty below,
packing everybody else's
but his own.

SUNDAY THE THIRTEENTH

Today I wear your mother's shirt.

I wish there were more to say,
but the day is ungenerous
and I don't know how to move
from your side of the bed.

All afternoon the shadows
reassure me that the sun
saw all angles of my face
as it left for tomorrow.

Now I wear dusk around my knees.

PHYSICS

What falls from the sky
is still deciding what it wants to be.
Something like rain, something like snow,
the streets mottled with wool caps and umbrellas.
Nevertheless, Ste. Catherine is soaked.
I hang my jacket, the added weight: proof of indecision.

The horns of snow trucks disharmonize
and someone else laughs, senses a poem.
Any minute now is my new repetend.
Any minute now for the water to boil.
Any minute now for the mailman.

No mail in a week and I am certain I don't exist.
Loneliness, once the enemy,
has since become acceptance.
It blusters in and as I get older,
becomes easier to identify:
a hand palpating an imaginary organ
that joins my heart to my stomach,
qualms to lethargy.

The shorter afternoons
and the forced optimism of my daily horoscope
make me seek approbation.
Today's reads:
Your job is to maximize the moment.
Quit judging yourself.

I pass an alley

and a voice from somewhere above me
calls out a curt *Sorry!*
I don't bother to look up.

What falls from the sky
is an apology
belonging to anyone who can hear it;
singing, *A woman left lonely will soon grow tired of waiting,*
a voice spread through that takes its time to dry.

BEGINNING AGAIN

Past the serried cottages,
the ice cracked over Muskoka Lake
and I only knew
because I wanted to be there.

I was nearly knocked back
into the glassed throat of the river
but there was only you and the sordid city
to remind me how dreams give out by morning.

When you opened your jacket,
I smelled daffodils. But none appeared,
just the palsied spring making promises
of a single April.

You tell me you're at an age
fit only for reasonable risks,
though we know it's not so much risk
as reason.

I'm dreaming of a snapped river,
the possibility that warm weather
will stun the world into melting,
pounce in to laugh
and stay.

My attempts at self-preservation
are winter leftovers,
inviting absurdity.

In the early light of a distant shore,
I find my name crinkled on your floor
and it didn't hurt a bit.

ANXIETY

The day starts
with a quick cast of a spoon into my mug,
the scooping of a tea bag
and its wet tumble into my empty cereal bowl.

The fixed call of a bird can take me anywhere.

To contemplate the day
after I stayed up with familiar friends,
the same ones who asked me when I was four,
What if the house burns down?
Who will save your family now?

Years later,
they are back to cradle me in the dark.
To speculate,
Maybe tonight the floors above will give.
You'll collapse into pieces.

I am glad to have made it through yesterday.
The steel-toed man beside me on the subway
scratched his lottery ticket with a pocket knife
and how easy it would have been then
to die.

I hold my mug with two hands.
Drink the darkness of the tea in one breath.

ORISON

a memory:

sleep
sliding off your body
a stray hair
you reach out I duck

you dream

of favourable interpretations

•

the vinous stain on your lips
as you whispered your prayers
gave a hazy sense of forgiveness —

did you believe then
that a woman,
epic as an armada,
could diminish

then be moored to your pier?

weeping alighted

on the grasshopper
clinging to the screen

the empty bottle
collecting dew

NOTES OUTSIDE YOUR WINDOW

Love arrives and dies in all disguises.
— Michael Ondaatje

I looked up at your window,
(so bright-eyed, poised and observant)
harmless
until you walked past.

How I wished I could mistake you for a stranger.

I watched the familiar bones of your hand
cup somebody else's yawn.

An ugly mouth with no right.
Those lips know no luck.

Then the window blinked.
A curtain swished a floral face:
two hanging pots for eyes,
their falling tendrils linked into a nose

the orchid on a table, a certain smile.

REQUIEM IN MAY

I.

May comes in a half-swallow
and rain gives in to tulips.

The world's reawakening
is its own way of saying,
Look about you.
Don't look so bewildered.

Even we didn't expect April to linger.

II.

Every morning,
I walk out and am greeted by a woman
with a scarf wrapped around her head.
She calls me by the name of her dead cat
and won't take her eyes off me.

Even then
it is difficult to be the disheartening *live*
for the anticipated *dead.*

There is enough disappointment already.
Needless to start wishing we're something
we're not.

III.

It rains throughout the night.
Under the dawn,
only the grass is effulgent.

Every day is confused for garbage day.

The grieving woman pokes at a stripped tire
with her cane,
prodding it as if it were roadkill.

The dead tulips in my garbage bag,
reach out a cool leaf
to touch my hand one last time.

ENCASEMENT

The park by our apartment
went missing beneath ice.
All that's left is the statue's shoulders.

Now you've gone under too,
ice-bound in the middle of the kitchen.

Outside, the empty bench
lends its space for snow
and a scatter of blue pigeons
peck and bob around it.
Some even alight on the statue,
still recognize the glint of the afternoon sun
like a beacon to navigate the frozen lake.

But inside
I can't make out any part of you:
dangerous shorelines of your body,
the pull of your shirt when you take a breath —
the same one I've been letting go to thaw you,
still too shallow to do any good.

FREESTANDING

The man on Queen Street
spends his days kneeling before a broken city,
cheating gravity as he builds towers
with bricks,
rocks and cinder blocks.

He can teach me something about balance.

On a day when the skies
are more tiring to reach
I will ask for my turn, look down,
watch him break and re-erect me
with goldenrods for kneecaps,
hair of sweetgrass,
insides flavoured like mint and promise.

The crowd will toss coins at my feet
and I will grow, tall as a ponderosa,
amidst his concrete, votive offering.

ALL HALLOWS

A cat drips mice blood on her paws.
I trail in the last season,
another city's salt still clinging to my boots.

There is no one way to learn a place.
I get lost. I memorize street names
but never turn into them.

I learn the scent of my home like a kitten.
Pluck me too soon from the nest,
and I am unable to orient myself.

October is not content with leaves
and shrivelling light. It wants us wrapping
our bloom around our necks and choking on it.

Another year finishes its turn, it says,
and a sandwich bag misses the garbage,
stays afloat for the rest of the day.

I give thanks . . .
Lifting my arms in the mirror,
I measure out the small muscles

that start where my ribs begin.
Two spoonfuls' worth.
Little curves only good for small offerings.

I've never stared at a mirror so closely.
The month has me wishing for the boy
of my adolescence.

Remember he who once loved you
to a point where you could disappear.
If you didn't exist, I would still invent you.

We build cities around these words,
a brick for every one of them.
We'll learn to call them homonyms.

When they are gone, collected in baskets,
their smell flung to greener sides,
we, like kittens, will simply wander in circles.

Unaccountable activities of my afternoons:
I peruse the classifieds, look for
who's giving away cats, or who's lost them.

I spy on neighbours from my balcony.
Once I saw two teenagers in the empty lot,
fettered and oblivious,

and I, just learning the delicacy between people,
the quiet that can stretch in two directions,
watched

the things we do to each other in empty lots,
the continuing war of ungrace and love
and a stray balanced on an iron fence for one second.

Their two young bodies lifted and never came down.
The cat, as usual, landed on her feet.
I circled another ad.

When the month slips away,
the snowplough's horn will replace it.
A herald's call.

Its ruckus and greasy motor
backing up into a stream of morning traffic,
its piercing yellow angled out of nowhere.

It drives the snow tumbling onto the sidewalk,
forming new mountains — the usual habit of gods —
while I collect the footprints of the homeless.

Tonight I will not win. Younger,
I pretended to be a witch with cut-out paper cats.
Now even younger will do.

Most everyone's mad here
and we hold mirrors up to our noses
to look down at the sky.

When all the night arrives,
we play cards. The stars cheat
and the moon repines its phases.

The streetlamps blink a song,
crooning first in major, then in minor,
sounding suddenly frightful.

HATCHLINGS

The crow wish'd every thing was black, the owl that every thing was white.
— William Blake

All month we wondered about birds.

Mornings spent spying
on the fowl with her set black stare,
our faces peering out your bathroom window
like two moons.

We marvelled at the nest,
the tenuous twigs and stems wreathed
into refuge, made entirely with no hands.

In your backyard,
the old stump glowered in the evening.
It was dying at an angle
before it was chopped down
and it will take a few more generations
for the birds to forget ghost limbs
and recall being born in air.

We've forgotten where we belong.
Sometimes we hear a bird scuffling,
trapped behind your kitchen wall,
and he must think he is nowhere close
to where he actually is.

When the eggs finally hatched,

I saw them alone, shivering,
wet downy things.
Before the mother flew in
I called out your name
and from the next room, you had to ask
because you couldn't recognize my voice.

Four

We can never be born enough.
— e. e. cummings

LOCUST

I've been struggling not to lose sight of myself
getting away as the evening sun
drags the shadows
deeper into the ground.
Yes, kick me out of your republic.
I have lied, boastful
but incapable
of pinning everything and nothing down
ten thousandfold.
However many ways to make one smile
is however many ways our lips can trickle into a grin,
however many dark corners
we duck into for that needed drag,
the many ways we clasp our hands when we pray.

NOTES & ACKNOWLEDGEMENTS

Some poems from this collection have been previously published, often in different forms and with different titles. I am grateful to the editors and staff of the following journals and anthologies: *Contemporary Verse 2*, *Ricepaper*, *Room*, *Matrix*, *The Toronto Quarterly*, *Headlight Anthology*, *echolocation*, *Prairie Fire*, *The Fevered Spring Anthology*, *bullpenned*, *Two Review*, *Asian Cha* and *pax americana*.

The title of this book is taken from a passage in Book VI of *The Aeneid* (Doubleday Anchor Books, 1952), translated by C. Day Lewis.

> "The flesh that is laden with death, the anatomy of clay:
> Whence these souls of ours feel fear, desire, grief, joy,
> But encased in their blind, dark prison discern not the heaven-light above."

The title of Part One comes from a note on the surrealists, displayed in the Art Gallery of Ontario: "They uncovered what lies at the core of human existence — the irrational urges to love, to desire and to destroy."

The sectional epigraphs for Part One–Three ("I affirmed that — for me — personality is a mystery; that mysteries alone are significant; and that love is the mystery-of-mysteries who creates them all") is from "nonlecture three: i & selfdiscovery" found in *i: six nonlectures* (Harvard University Press, 1981) by e. e. cummings.

The sectional epigraph for Part Four ("We can never be born enough") is from "nonlecture four: i & you & is" found in *i: six nonlectures* by e. e. cummings.

Page 9: "Roses"
The epigraph is from Stephen Dunn's poem, "Imagining Myself My Father."

Page 29: "Insomniac Conjectures"
The lines from Wallace Stevens are from his poem, "Gubbinal."

Page 31: "Delilah in Seven Parts"
This piece received Honourable Mention in the 2008 Quebec Writing Competition (Quebec Writers' Federation).

Page 38: "Elegy I"
This poem is in memory of Manmohan Chandra Sharma (1948–2009).

Page 50: "First Hymn"
The epigraph is from "Cædmon's Hymn."

Page 61: "Crossing Borders"
The epigraph is from Book IV of *The Aeneid*. ["... I recognize the traces of the olden flame."]

Page 63: "Dead-walking"
The epigraph is from Mary di Michele's poem, "A Poem for My Daughter."

Page 70: "Blood Sign #2"
This poem is a response to Ana Mendieta's same titled performance as watched on film (1974, 1 minute).

Page 84: "Notes Outside Your Window"
The epigraph is from "The Nine Sentiments" by Michael Ondaatje.

Page 93: "Hatchlings"
The epigraph is from "Proverbs of Hell" by William Blake.

Page 97: "Locust"
This poem is a response to William Carlos Williams' poem, "The Pink Locust" in *Journey to Love* (Random House, 1955).

•

I am grateful to everyone at ECW Press for their enthusiasm and hard work. Special thanks to Rob Winger for his care and insight. My sincerest gratitude to my editor, Michael Holmes, for his close attention, expertise and steadfast commitment to fine-tuning this book. I am thankful to those who first saw the manuscript and were encouraging. Thank you, too, to John Steffler and our workshop for seeing some of these poems when they were at their most naked. Warmest thanks to my friends for their kindness, good humour and continued support. Love to my family, my brothers, Edmond and Edwin, and my parents.

This book is for S., about whom I can never say quite enough.